The Ridgeway

By

Tess Glanville

And

Michele Rumsey

Intro

Have you ever wanted to chuck your horses onto a lorry and set off on a wonderful adventure with them?

For many years I had this dream of riding The Ridgeway (an ancient track that runs from Overton Hill in Wiltshire to Ivinghoe Beacon in Buckinghamshire). The old track is 87 miles long on foot, and about 120 miles on horseback (due to horses not being allowed on a part of the Ridgeway).

For a long time, I ran the Hollesley branch of RDA (Riding for The Disabled), and one blustery March day, my crazy friend Tess and I were throwing around fund raising ideas. We wanted to raise a couple of grand, so we could turn some ugly pig-sties into a decked garden area for wheelchair users to hang out in the Summer .... Instead of risking being mown down by a pony and trap while sitting in the yard.

We had recently been donated a pile of ball dresses circa 1982! The donator thought we could sell them. We thought we had more chance of selling bags of dust! And so, we began to think how we could use them.

Next thing you know we had decided to ride my ponies the length of the Ridgeway....wearing the hideous dresses. I have no idea how we came up with that! And so, we embarked on the long journey of planning.

Tess started a brilliant Blog, so the first half of this book is all hers, still in the Blog form it was written. For years I have thought we should write up the days of the adventure in a longer more detailed form, lest we forgot. Not much chance of that! Every minute is still etched on my memory, so the second part of the book is mine.

So... If you have ever wanted to chuck your Horses on a lorry and set off on a wonderful adventure with them......read on.

Part One

The Blog

This first part is The Blog that Tess wrote, mostly about the planning that went into our journey. I have copied it in Blog Form as it was written.

A) Because it is funny.

And

B Because we were stupid... Or Naïve.

However, we completed our goal, so it just goes to show... any idiot can do this!!

About the Horses

Michele and Tess from Hollesley RDA are planning to do a sponsored ride along The Ridgeway in aid of Riding for The Disabled Association. Dressed in Ballgowns!

They need all the help they can get! Can you help in anyway? They have the horses and the dresses! They need transport, diesel, and anything else you can think of. Oh Yes, And Sponsorship!!

The Horses

Paddy (The Black one)

Is a 13-year-old gelding. Probably a Fell. He is 14.2hh with lots of personality and a broad (wicked?) sense of humour. He's used for RDA, where he is a star. Out on hacks is another story though! Pet hates include pigs, cattle and garden ornaments.

He's done well in local competitions and is a demon over cross country.

The Ridgeway will be his swansong, after which he gets to take it easy (although he may have a different opinion).

Ryscheyed (The Grey)

Is a 14.2hh, 8-year-old Arab gelding. He's a real muck magnet and a typical Arab. Occasionally a bit of a drama queen, he often looks to Paddy as an example, which can be interesting. He is bred for endurance and has a spectacular turn of speed (and a hell of a buck), so the ride should be a breeze for him.

Sunday, April 15, 2007

Models

We have a photographer from The East Anglian Daily Times coming tomorrow, so we thought it was about time the boys (Paddy and Ryscheyed) had their spring baths. They are pretty scruffy and hairy after a winter in rugs. Ryscheyed in particular is a right muck monster.... Typical grey! It was the perfect day for it, so of course we changed our minds and went for a ride instead. Well, we do need to get them fit, not to mention us. They would only have rolled anyway!

So, it's up at stupid o' clock tomorrow morning for a shampoo and set to make them look pretty. Hopefully they will both behave themselves and not make us look like complete pillocks!

Monday, May 7, 2007
We Are Famous!

I'm posting this a bit late as I've spent the last couple of weeks acquiring a healthy patina of ingrained dirt while sailing up from Spain.

As you can see, we made it into the local paper (and narrowly missed flattening the photographer).

All we need now are the offers of money to start rolling in. Contact us if you are feeling generous.

Paddy and Ryscheyed have had a lovely relaxing bank holiday weekend, boy are they in for a shock tomorrow!!

East Anglian news online at www.eadt.co.uk

Charity riders having a ball

Wednesday, May 9, 2007

Wet and Windy

After quite a long rest, we resumed the boys' fitness programme. With perfect timing, after a fine morning, it blew up a Hooley and started raining as soon as we set out. The boys were not best pleased. They had the wind up their tails from the start, prancing around and snorting at everything.

We let Ryscheyed choose the route, inexplicably he chose to go through the dump. In the interests of their ongoing education, we let them. A bloke was dumping stuff from a truck, which was the scariest thing they had seen in a long time (though some bricks came a close second).

Then we had to make it past the irrigator.... which took a while. Just when we thought they had settled we were confronted with a bouncy castle, complete with screaming kids!

Having negotiated that with the expected snorting and spooking, we met some little mares in a field.

Paddy felt the need to strut his stuff, though the effect was somewhat spoilt when he shied at a rabbit. Hopefully both the weather and their behaviour will improve tomorrow.

Thursday, May 10, 2007

Still Raining....

Well it's still raining and windy, so we decided to school the boys today. Ryscheyed started well, until Paddy joined us, and he felt the need to really show off. He's got the most fantastic paces, but there are limits!

Paddy took one look at the indoor school and decided he was (bridle) lame. Poor baby! I took Rash over a little jump a few times, lovely jump once he figures out what he is supposed to do with it. Shell didn't jump Paddy, just in case he really was lame, but worked on suppling exercises instead.

Eventually the rain stopped hammering on the roof, so we went for a short walk. They both behaved liked a pair of dobbins until we pointed them towards home.

Still hoping the weather will improve, although the ground is still very hard after the recent dry spell, and a bit greasy due to the sudden rain.

I think we are getting the March winds and April showers all in one go! Farrier and Dentist on Monday, lucky boys!

If anyone out there has any pearls of wisdom to offer on The Ridgeway itself, we would love to hear from you.

Ta

Friday, May 11, 2007

More Rain

Filthy weather again today. We couldn't face another soaking, so decided to give the boys the day off.

Instead we spent all afternoon on the phone, arranging (or trying to arrange) horse accommodation for the ride. We are still looking for somewhere in the areas of Nettlebed, Wendover and Aldbury.

Suggestions anyone?

Saturday, May 12, 2007

Another Day, Another Deluge

Undaunted (?) by the rain and gales we decided to hack the boys out today. Actually, they were pretty good considering, although we were overtaken by a power walker! The weather was so grim that they failed to notice an assortment of farm machinery and a couple of irrigators. The pheasant was pretty scary though.

Sunday, May 13, 2007
More #@$$%# Rain!

Yes, it's STILL raining in Sunny Suffolk. We will soon be needing an amphibious vehicle to get to the yard. Ryscheyed got a day off today, being an Arab, he doesn't seem quite so prone to lard. Paddy on the other hand is noticeably tubby, so no rest for him. Foolishly I moved the boys' fence back before catching him, but we got there in the end.

Had a good hack with a decent bit of a gallop now the tracks aren't like concrete. It was a good experience for him as we met horses (very alarming), pigs (smell and noise only), black sheep with BIG horns, and finally cattle. Apart from a bit of snorting he was pretty good about it all.

I really must repair the hole in my chaps though. Got a big soggy patch. Mind you, pretty much all of me is a big soggy patch.

Monday, May 14, 2007

No News

Unless more wind and rain counts? We had the Farrier today for all horses (13 in total), not to mention the Vet for Tetanus jabs and Teeth Rasping! So, we have been too busy to ride.

We also moved all the horses onto Summer grazing, possibly more in hope than expectation given the weather.

Paddy will be doing an RDA session tomorrow.... Pics to follow.

Tuesday, May 15, 2007
Hectic Day and MORE Rain

Tuesdays are always busy at the yard. Driving in the morning, Riding and Driving in the afternoon and an Evening session as well.

This combined with the delightful weather meant no hack for the boys. Despite this, Ryscheyed managed to exercise himself. Finding himself alone (I.e. without God, well Paddy actually) he tore round the field doing the whole Arab thing, head tossing, sliding stops.... In fact, there was only electric tape between him and Blue (a driving Cob), but hey, that's Rash for you!

Having got himself thoroughly lathered up; he then had a lovely roll.

Paddy on the other hand was engaged in the serious business of being an RDA pony....

Wednesday, May 16, 2007

Three's A Crowd

A (brief) window of opportunity with the weather, so we went for a shortish hack. Normally the boys go as a pair. I can't imagine why people don't want to join us....

Today was an exception, three whole people wanted to come too. We thought it would be a useful experience for them, although we did wonder if Paddy might think he was out hunting. It's been ages since Rash has been out in company, so he was a bit of an unknown quantity.

In the event both of them behaved immaculately (more than can be said for some of the others). As we had novice riders with us, we took it gently, and amazingly nothing went wrong. A complete absence of spooking, bucking or bolting. Paddy lost a shoe (at the furthest point from home of course), but he didn't let it slow him down.... Not when he could be showing off in front of a mare.

If there is anyone out there who would like to join us for a section of The Ridgeway, you are more than welcome.

Our dates are as follows:

Sun 15 July, Overton Hill to Ogbourne St George (departing around 2pm)

Mon 16 July, Ogbourne St George to Sparsholt Down (early start)

Tues 17 July, Sparsholt Down to Streatley (early start)

Weds 18 July, Streatley to Watlington (early start)

Thurs 19 July, Watlington to Wendover (early start)

Fri 20 July, Wendover to Aldbury (the Bridleway ends here, so we intend to carry on to Ivinghoe Beacon on foot, but still in costume

Tuesday, May 29, 2007

Update

It seems every time I put foot on dry land the weather turns! I've been away at sea for a week, not warm, but sunshine and light winds. I come ashore and what happens? Hurricane Hell!! The boys are back in rugs, despite it being almost June.

Shell took Paddy out during the week, on his own down to the River. He was in a spooky mood, so she wasn't thrilled to see a field of cattle ahead. Fortunately, they were on the other side of the Creek. She managed to persuade Paddy past them (by pointing out that there was a Creek between them and anyway, he should feel sorry for them as they were destined to become burgers...). Anyway, it worked!

The sponsorship is starting to come in, but don't let that hold you back... We need More!!

Saturday, June 2, 2007

Pub Crawl

Hooray, it's NOT raining! In the interests of publicising the ride locally and educating the boys we thought it would be a good idea to hack down to the local pub. Being very well organised (?) we even checked beforehand that there were people there. My daughter Kathy volunteered to drive and meet us, along with her sister Ellie, and Mickey.

So much for plans, she got there first and it was closed.

Having gone to the trouble of dressing up and frightening the pants off Rash with the voluminous skirt we decided to carry on regardless. The boys were as good as gold on the way to the Pub, even when a bus passed us at close quarters (Ok Rash sat down, but you couldn't blame him really). Sure enough the Pub was still closed, so we took the decision to carry on to the next one. Rather more education than we intended, but good experience all the same.

We took a route neither of the boys had seen before, passing an assortment of horses, flappy fencing, machinery and general junk. We got a steady canter going (Yes, I was hanging onto Rash's' head, there's no way he was getting a chance to buck with that skirt!!). No major incidents, we met some very helpful walkers who redirected us to the Pub when we were lost and thirsty. Some lovely views on the way. The boys attracted a fair amount of attention when we got to the Pub, particularly from small girls. Not sure what they made of us!

On the way back we called into the previously closed Pub, where Scrumpy (Shells Jack Russell) had pulled the table over, soaking Kathy and Mickey in beer, before running off to the dining room.

As we arrived to this chaos, a troupe of Morris Dancers erupted from the Pub, causing the Boys to become over excited! We quickly deposited them in the Horse Park round the back.

I don't think anyone in the Pub missed our arrival!!

Surprisingly a nice lady gave us £4.

So, Hello to anyone we met today and Thanks to those that promised us sponsorship.

And Thanks to Diana Fenton with whom we will be staying on the 17th, for the lovely helpful letter (and offer of breakfast). Anyone else feeling kind?

Sunday, June 3, 2007

Sunny! And That ****** Dress

Yes, I know I keep going on about the weather, but having sun and a lack of rain and gales is Wonderful!

We went for a sedate hack today. The boys seemed a little shell-shocked after yesterdays' experience. Even Paddy's' obligatory 'snort and jog' routine was very half-hearted.

We took them on a familiar route (one where we come around a corner and straight into canter) ... Couldn't be bothered. Just as well as the grass is waist high so you can't see the rabbit holes and ruts. Even a herd of cattle and a flock of geese (all in one go) failed to elicit so much as a twitch. We are thinking of selling them on to Trekking Centre when this is over (Sorry Boys, just joking).

I have decided I am NOT wearing that dress!

The faster we went yesterday, the lower the dress got, to the point where it had descended to my waist, with the added bonus of trapping my arms. Fortunately, I wore a vest (the World just isn't ready for that view). Shells' dress is far more sensible, having a shoulder strap, and she has something to hold it up with! Alterations (my dress is also about 9 inches too long, and fits me like a sack) and straps will be happening soon.

We will also both be having splits up the front of the skirts for ease of mounting and dismounting.... And not having acres of fabric bunched up in front of us.

Tuesday, June 12, 2007
One of Those Days

Having just got back from Ireland, where we had a week of scorching weather...... Yes, I am obsessed, I was all ready to carry on as usual.

Paddy in particular is nowhere near fit (apparently, he has lost the will to play up after the pub excursion).

No such luck. It seems we no longer have a Lorry as it has spontaneously (?) disintegrated, so much of today has been sucking up, hinting and pleading with anyone we know who might be able to lend us one. No luck so far, but we haven't tried everyone we know, and we live in hope. It seems everyone is busy with shows that week. BIG HINT!!! If anyone has a lorry Please, Please, Please, get in touch.

Just in case the Lorry disaster isn't enough, we simply cannot find anywhere for the horses on the night of the 18th. We will be in the Watlington Area, and despite what the guide books say there is no stabling or grazing to be found.... At least not by us.

Another BIG HINT: Does anyone out there know of a smallish patch of grass where we can park the Boys? We don't need a big field and will bring electric fencing is necessary.

HELP? If we can't find anywhere, we will have to do 40 miles in one day!

Wednesday, June 13, 2007

Update on Lorry Etc

At some point, we might get to give the horses some proper exercise, when we can stop running around like headless chickens trying to find a Lorry. We tried a few more people today, lots of helpful suggestions, but still no Lorry. Desperate measures being called for, we contacted the local radio (BBC Radio Suffolk) and asked them to broadcast an appeal. Watch this space.

As for the exercise, a quick spin around the River Wall was all we managed at the end of the day. It's so overgrown that we didn't want to risk anything faster than a brisk trot.... A pace which Ryscheyed in particular has difficulty in getting his head round. I mean, why trot when you can ponce around in canter?

Paddy has started to show signs of life again, particularly when he was snorted at through the hedge by a large cow.

We are planning to do another Pub Crawl this Saturday, probably to The Sorrell Horse and Ramsholt Arms again, and perhaps The Alderton Swan if we think we can make it.

This time we will be shaking tins, so make sure you have change handy (notes will do to of course).

On my way to Ireland last week I stopped off in Streatley and Goring to have a look at what awaits us. Having read a description of Goring as a 'market town' we were a little concerned that it might be a teeming metropolis. Fortunately, this is not the case, although it's not short of traffic. Actually, it's quite picturesque, I just hope the Boys think so too and don't attempt a reprise of Becher's Brook as we cross the bridge.

This is where the Ridgeway stops being a Bridleway and becomes a footpath. We will need to go on to Swans Way, and then The Icknield Way. I hunted for signs of Swans Way, but only found The Ridgeway and The Thames Path. I asked a few locals including the Lock Keeper.... Nobody seems to know. Confused? We will be!

Thursday, June 14, 2007

Panic!

More of the headless chicken routine today, playing 'Hunt the Lorry'. Debs managed to go live on SGR (local radio) to beg for one. Still awaiting results on that.

We have suckered her into being interviewed on BBC Radio Suffolk tomorrow (Sorry Debs) … Listen out after 11.30am tomorrow. We will get there eventually, even if we have to strap skateboards to their hooves and tow them!!

After much phone wrangling, we finally managed to get out for a ride. It had become pleasantly cool after a very sweaty day; Paddy was certainly happier.

More brisk trotting, which Ryscheyed is still not convinced by, Paddy seems to be developing a fifth gait... Incredibly uncomfortable super-fast trot, occasionally breaking into canter. He's usually like sitting on a (somewhat bouncy) armchair. This is a revolting development.

Friday, June 15, 2007

Living in Hope

Well Debs made it live onto BBC Radio Suffolk, and a fine job of it she made too. She is now our official PR Person... Although she may not know this (yet). So, the plea has gone out, again, make with the Lorry!!

Horse wise it has been a bit windier today, a pleasant relief from the mugginess. Pads is gradually waking up and showing signs of enjoying himself again. We went for a decent enough hour and a half hack, nowhere especially challenging. The going is pretty good at the moment, with just the right amount of rain.

Rash was brilliant at the gates (which he did have an issue with), he did however have a couple of moments. Once when I turned around and put my hand on his bum. Anyone would have thought the hounds of Hades had just landed on him.

Then I went to get something from my pocket, obviously it was highly dangerous!

He shot forward with his nose in the air (his well-known Llama impression).

Pads being made of sterner stuff, only slammed the brakes on, and spun, when a flock of pigeons flapped out of a wheat field. Perhaps they were vultures in disguise. Who knows? Still we made it all the way home in one piece and they must be getting fitter as neither sweated up, despite trotting and cantering most of the way.

Thanks to Juliette Dean in Dunsmore who has kindly agreed to put the Boys up on the 19th, and to everyone who has been helpful and generous with information and advice.

Saturday, June 16, 2007

Discretion Being the Better Part of Valour

The Plan for today had been to hack to a few local pubs (again in full regalia). Naturally the weather conspired against us, the sun being too good to last. The thunder and lightning and downpour started just as we got the Boys in. We reckoned that not too many people would be inclined to sit outside a pub in these conditions, so we dashed out for a quick canter down by the River between showers.

Despite the ominous looking clouds and hefty gusts, the Boys were bordering on the somnambulistic. The herd of cattle failed to catch their attention at all. The steps up to the River Wall however, earned a good snorting from Paddy. Rash was bowling along nicely, until he was brought to an abrupt standstill... By a clump of grass!

No news about a Lorry yet, so we are working on Plan B (Or is that C? Or D?)

Sunday, June 17, 2007

Personal Trainer?

Paddy has a new personal trainer! My husband Alex. As Shell was busy with Father's Day stuff, I persuaded him (against his better judgement), to come out with us on his beloved bike.

Much to his surprise nothing horrible happened. Having someone to open gates is very handy, he was also useful for exploring the more unlikely (overgrown) looking bits of Bridleway, and rescuing a small dog from Paddy's' wrath (Pads really hates having his heels snapped at).

Alex couldn't understand what all the fuss about Paddy's' reputation as a fire breathing, snorting, prancing performance artist was all about... Until we met some strange horses! He certainly got out of the way quick enough, falling off his bike in the process (twice). Pads seemed to think he was another horse, didn't want to be separated from him, to the point where he was so close, Alex was being shoved into a ditch. They are best friends now.

Monday, June 18, 2007

Bridleway? What Bridleway?

The reason Rash is looking a little cheesed off in the photo below might have something to do with where we took himself and Paddy today. Thinking a little roadwork would not be out of order, we headed for the cut through onto the road. It's an official bridleway, signposts and all! The start was less than auspicious with nettles up to their shoulders, but it's usually ok that way so we persevered. Unfortunately, we persevered beyond the point of no return.

Having ploughed our way through even higher nettles, we found we could go no further, and had to ride through a potato field. Paddy was not a happy boy as he sank to his hocks a few times. We eventually found a footpath, which although not ideal, was the lesser of two evils.

Sincerely hoping the Ridgeway is better maintained than this, as we might not have survived the experience with Ball-gowns to contend with as well.

We made it home safely in the end and I don't think the Boys were too traumatised after all. Our dogs (who will NOT be accompanying us on the ride due to the complete inability to understand the command "Come here you little *******") were wondering where we had got to though.

Tuesday, June 19, 2007
Thank You, Thank You, Thank You

We have got a trailer!! Ok so it's not a lorry, but it's a means of getting to the start of the ride, and a good solid trailer it is, new floor too. The panic isn't quite over as we still have to find something to tow it with, but it's a damn good start.

HUGE THANK-YOU to Amanda x

Due to all the chasing around we didn't ride today, but Paddy in particular could probably do with a break (we don't want him to die on us, before or during the ride). It's a fine balance and we are probably erring on the side of caution.

Just so no-one forgets why we are doing this; I've included a pic from tonight's' RDA session.

The kids are practising an obstacle course which they will be doing for real on 14th July, along with a dressage test.

The Pony is Silver, a Shetland Pony on loan to us from Theresa Buchannon.

And this is Bridie, a dear little Sec A, belonging to Moya Luddington.

Wednesday, June 20, 2007

Hop-A-Long

Nothing dramatic today. Busy but routine at the Yard. We may have a van and a driver, but I don't want to say too much in case I jinx it!

There were magnificent thunderstorms here last night. I was looking out of my bedroom window at the Lightning, thinking, 'Please don't hit the horses'. Puddles and lakes everywhere today, so the going was nice and soft. It's at times like these you appreciate the sandy ground.

Paddy was painfully stiff at first, but loosened up after the first mile or so. Shell is beginning to suspect that he's trying it on. Bit of a Catch 22 really. Rash was Rash, as usual. His trot is getting a lot more even, less of the acceleration, deceleration, acceleration....

A large puddle turned out to be the scariest thing we had seen for weeks though. He was well on his way home before I managed to pull him up (perhaps he saw his reflection?)

The rest of the hack was quiet enough, though we may have scared a Bus Driver.... I reckon he thought Rash was trying to rear because of the Bus. But the truth is, he had got distracted by the Bus and inadvertently stood in a puddle!

Paddy was very quiet, apart from shooting out into the road when he saw the Pub garden ornaments (for the 100th time).

Hop-Along 2, And Other Stories

Not a lot to report from Yesterday (mostly because I was in Hospital.... Nothing to do with the Horses!).

Fliss came and looked at Paddy (She does Backs), and came to the conclusion that he had wrenched his hip when he sank into the potato field. She did her stuff on him, but he has to have a couple of days off.

Rash had a lesson and apparently, he was pretty good, although working in the School must have come as a bit of a shock after the last few weeks of happy hacking.

Today was time to start loading practise with the trailer. Pads strolled on and stuck his nose straight in the bucket of carrots.

Rash has a 'thing' about trailers, so we weren't expecting miracles. We took it all very quietly, no pressure, no fuss.

Managed to get two feet inside the trailer (briefly). This was actually a bit of a result as we have spent hours with him refusing to even set a foot on the ramp.

Thanks again the Amanda, now we have something to practise with.

Hopefully we are going to get dressed up and make idiots of ourselves in Woodbridge tomorrow. We have a 'Begging Licence' and will be bringing a cute harmless pony with us, rather than risking the boys freaking out and causing havoc!

If you come and point and laugh... Please donate as well.

Saturday, June 23, 2007

Begging!!

Today we got all dressed up and took Bridie to Woodbridge (complete with a begging permit from the council). First, we had to pick up our transport (trailer and Landy) from Poplar Park Equestrian Centre, Hollesley. On the way, we found ourselves under a cracker of a thunderstorm... This did not bode well for our fundraising effort. However, by the time we had got Bridie ready and loaded, the deluge had abated.

Shell and myself met Ellie (my daughter) and Alex (our photographer for the day) and off we headed into town. Bridie was all dolled-up with ribbons, and behaved like the saint she is. We dragged her up the main street, while Ellie demanded money with menaces from unsuspecting passers-by (very politely of course, and who can resist a child with a cute pony??).

Quite a few people recognised Bridie and lots of people, little girls in particular came to say hello.

We certainly attracted plenty of attention (Two grown women and a child dressed in 1700's type dresses, and a fairy pony... Even in Woodbridge, this is odd!). There were times when I was afraid, we might be the cause of a car crash! We even got smiles and waves from a Bus Driver and his passengers.

Up on Market Hill, we ran into a Film Crew, or something like it. We told them what we were up to, and allowed them to film us, but clean forgot to ask them what they were doing (If it was you, and you read this, do tell, please).

We met loads of nice people who were interested in what we were doing, and generous with it. Thank you to everyone, we raised £114.40 today!!

Still looking for more donations of course!

Finished the day with another downpour. Perfect timing!!

Begging in Town

Wednesday, June 27, 2007

Back in Action?

Well Paddy has had his R and R, and is now fit to be ridden again. He was much more like himself on yesterdays' hack, the old Paddy bounce is back. Of course, the weather is doing us no favours at all, timing is everything if we don't want a soaking. On the ride itself we won't have a choice, but right now there is no point undergoing unnecessary hardship.

We are still in a bit of a limbo situation with the transport. There is a vital piece missing from the trailer, which we are hoping will turn up any day now (although it will be redundant if we can't persuade Rash onto the damn thing!). Still haven't got a definite towing vehicle, but we live in hope.

There is a very dodgy picture of us on the Front Page of the local newsletter, but hopefully it won't put anyone off giving us money!

Thursday, June 28, 2007
Eureka!! Sort Of

It's been a somewhat frustrating day. Hectic all morning (when the weather was reasonable). When things eased off in the afternoon it would have been nice to go for a hack, but guess what?

Paddy is losing a shoe!! I thought it sounded loose a while ago and the Farrier tweaked it (he didn't have time to replace both fore's). However, it's now more of a Flip-Flop. As he's already a little unlevel it's not worth risking a nail through the sole, or any strain from working him without the shoe (he has a tendency to be a little 'footy' anyway).

We decided the most productive use of time would be for Shell to lunge Paddy in the school, while I tried to persuade Rash that the trailer wasn't going to eat him!

Apparently, Pads isn't entirely sound, not tracking up with his near hind in trot, though it didn't stop him bucking in canter! He generally loosens up if you work him through it, so here's hoping.

Rash still has some reservations about the trailer. We spent half an hour with me sitting in it with a bucket of feed while he decided whether or not he could cope with the ramp.

We thought he was being a stubborn git. Having said that, when we worked out how to move the partition over, he loaded in less than a minute (though he looked a little surprised to find himself there). Claustrophobic!

This leaves us with a dilemma. He will load if he can go on first, but will undoubtedly throw a fit if we try and move the partition to make room for Paddy. Oh Dear....

The bottom line is WE STILL NEED A LORRY!!! Someone, somewhere must have one they can spare for a week? Please help us, or this ride may never happen...

Friday, June 29, 2007
Donner Und Blitzen

More Thunderstorms!! We may have to put flippers on the Boys at this rate. Paddy's' shoe has finally dropped off. Irritating but not unexpected. The good news on that front is that there is no damage with it, we just have to wait for Stuart (the Farrier) to turn up on Tuesday. With the weather forecast the way it is, this isn't such a blow.

The other good news is that Rash is overcoming his trailer induced nervous breakdown quite nicely. Walked on with hardly any hesitation today. There's still a way to go, but we are definitely getting there. Ok he flattened me on his way off... But never mind.

The Bad News is that our own nervous breakdowns are still in full flight. STILL NO DAMN LORRY! We must have phoned and begged most Suffolk's' Lorry owning population today. Still nothing. I will be at Fynn Valley Horse Trials at Poplar Park on Sunday, dressed like a twit and begging pitifully for a Lorry.

Saturday, June 30, 2007

Real Life

Oh, My aching brain! As the weather shows no significant signs of improvement, both Shell and I, left the horses alone and had a day of normality (?). What that really means is that we both tried to stuff a weeks' worth of anything that doesn't involve horses into a day. We are both pretty shattered, not to mention stressed (yes, the Lorry, or lack of). We are now at the point where we need to be sorting out a list of things to bring and generally make sure everything is organised to run smoothly... Anyone out there want an unpaid job? What we really want is to have a few drinks and sleep for 24 hours! Ain't gonna happen!!

A day of poncing around the Horse Trials at Poplar Park, dressed like a complete *******
beckons tomorrow.

Bet it thrashes it down. Please show pity, offer me a Lorry, and lots of money??

Sunday, July 1, 2007
Jubilation!!

Today, as promised I made a pillock of myself. Hanging around a Horse Trials dressed in a Ballgown does absolutely nothing for ones' self-esteem. I spent 3 or 4 hours there, trying to maintain an expression of interested approachability. I suspect that what I achieved was an expression of near psychotic boredom.

On the plus side, it didn't rain (much) and I managed to collect £22. I did feel (while begging and whining for a Lorry) that the time should have been spent with the horses.

HOWEVER,

A lovely kind lady called Sue Crane phoned after I had given up and gone home AND OFFERED US A LORRY!! THANK YOU, SUE!! Apparently, it's called The Turd (due to its' colour).

It sounds like the Ritz though, luxury living for the Horse owner on the road! Our gratitude and relief knows no bounds.

By the time I left the Trials, both myself and Shell were in a state of despair, but that's all changed.

Now we can concentrate properly on getting the horses and ourselves ready.

Thanks, are also due to Mike Lloyd for allowing me to use their secretary's' tent today.

There are some wonderful people out there.

Monday, July 2, 2007

Silly!!

Rain and more rain!! Spent today doing publicity stuff... And a little shopping!!

This will be the bottom half of our 'Off Duty/Under the Dresses' outfits!! Tasteful eh??

We have also been thinking about bits and pieces we need, now we can stop thinking about a Lorry (Thanks again Sue, Sorry if this is getting boring now).

Any donations gratefully received.

The List is as follows:

2 x Bales of Haylage

2 x Bales of Shavings

Baby Wipes x lots (great for everything)

Ibuprofen x lots

Windproof Lighters x 2

Ariat Riding Trainers size 5 (Ahem!)

Crepe Bandages X 2 (for us)

Sticking Plasters

Liquid Skin

Purple Spray

Hoof Moist

Antiseptic Cream

Antihistamine Cream

Sudocream

Ice-cream (Joking!!)

Sunscreen (High Factor for Horses)

Surgical Spirit

Saline

Salt/Electrolyte

Electric Tape and posts (still haven't found Horse B'n'B for the 18th)

And anything else you can think of....

Calling all Nutters... If anyone out there wants to join us on a mountain bike we'd love to see you. We have a volunteer for the first leg (Cheers Nige). A spare pair of hands is a Godsend for opening gates, talking to people when the Boys are fidgeting, nipping into shops for emergency chocolate supplies and so on.

So is anyone fancies a somewhat more eventful than usual bike ride, please get in touch. There is a chance of a bed for the night if you need it.

It will be a laugh. Go on, Go on, Go on...

Optional Ballgowns provided! Go on, Go on, Go on.... I have some people in mind already, you know who you are!

Tuesday, July 3, 2007

OMG It's A Giant Raspberry

Interesting Title! But first WILL THE COMEDIAN DOING THE RAIN DANCE PLEASE STOP!!!

The weather continues to be dramatically awful. This morning was pleasant enough, but as usual that's the busy time. As soon as the clients had left, the skies darkened (cue dramatic music). Stuart the Farrier arrived, although I'm sure there's no connection!

His comment on our new jodhs was "OMG, It's a Giant Raspberry!"

Flattery was never his strong point. We were prepared to forgive him though because a) both horses are now fully shod for free, and b) he has given us a very generous donation. THANK YOU, STUART DURRANT.

Having now got two fully shod horses we were hoping for a hack at last. No such luck. Mega thunderstorm arrived; the skies lit up and the windows shook.

We opted for a schooling session in the end, although the power kept cutting out and leaving us in the dark.

Lightning strike in the field next to the Yard! Pads was deeply unimpressed by the whole thing. Rash seemed unbothered, although he kept knocking over cones as if they weren't there.

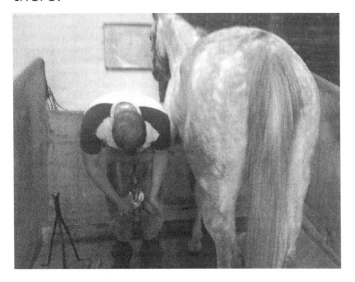

Wednesday, July 4, 2007

Itinerary Reminder

A quick reminder for anyone that wants to join us on bikes, horses or whatever... Or just come to gawp.

Sun 15 July, Overton Hill to Ogbourne St George – departing approx. 2pm.

Mon 16 July, Ogbourne St George to Sparsholt Down (early start).

Tues 17 July, Sparsholt Down to Streatley (early start)

Wed 18 July, Streatley to Watlington (early start)

Thur 19 July, Watlington to Wendover (early start)

Fri 20 July, Wendover to Aldbury (the Bridleway ends here, so we intend to carry on to Ivinghoe Beacon on foot, but still in costume).

It's not too long to go now. The rain/thunder/lightning has held off today, so the Boys finally got out in the fresh air. Paddy's' movement is much looser, for which we are thoroughly relieved.

Rash is now a little under the weather, with a bit of a cough and a snotty nose. Nothing dramatic though (possibly due to him munching on his bedding of old straw).

We had a bit of a canter, and I got up off his back for the first time in months. It was done with some trepidation as this is when he usually has his bucking fit.

He didn't put a foot wrong, almost a schoolmaster!

Thursday, July 5, 2007

Haircut and Other News

Relatively fine weather, Whoopee!! Sadly, we have to leave the little doggies behind, no matter how cute and appealing they are. Buffy always does her best to make me feel bad for abandoning her. However, we are hard-hearted... And they have a comfy Community Room to lounge around in.

Before we could leave, Paddy was in dire need of a haircut. He looks so much better Hogged, and was beginning to resemble a Bog Brush with extra hairy bits.

Paddy used to have a deep-seated antipathy to being clipped, to the point where he was dangerous. Shell tried everything, including sedation. In the end, a quiet persistence paid off and now he's just bored by the whole thing.

Rash is (was) appalled at the idea of clippers anywhere near him, he even hated having his feathers trimmed by hand. I did wonder if he would take exception to having to stand next to Pads while he was being done. But he wasn't bovvered! Trekking Centre here we come!

In fact, he was so chilled he let Shell trim his feet with the clippers! Pads was delighted with his new look, full of himself and back on form, jogging and revving up on the corners. It's great to see him enjoying himself again.

Rash is still not on top form; traces of snot remain. He has developed an interesting technique.... Wait till I come off his back in canter, then have a coughing fit (while still cantering). I hasten to add that I am not abusing the poor boy. I only asked for a gentle trot, but he keeps getting faster. Obviously not at deaths door yet.

Just over a week to go now!! Are we nervous??

Well.......Maybe!!

And Finally, ...

THANKS to Pip Greenwood from Hemcore who has offered us hemp bedding for our escapade.

Friday, July 6, 2007

Paddy is Definitely Back on Form

Paddy is back on form!!! We were worried he had lost his 'Paddiness', but no! The spring is definitely back in his step.

Picked up the bedding that Hemcore have kindly donated, and put some down in Paddy's' stable to see what he thinks of it. He wandered (well barged really) through the door and took a huge mouthful. It took a few moments for him to register that we hadn't been careless with the Chaff... His expression of disgust as he tried to spit it out was comical.

We hacked out again today, expecting all round spookiness due to the wind. Initially they were a pair of dobbins, but as we speeded up things got a little more interesting.

We found a great big tractor and a pile of huge crates at the end of a track. Rash was not amused and slammed the brakes on. Paddy was a bit braver, but also a bit circumspect.

They half passed along opposite sides of the crates, snorting and rolling their eyes. Formation riding after fashion. The blue plastic containers on the other side nearly caused a Paddy 'Spin and Bolt', but Shell pulled him up mid spin, as we collapsed in a fit of giggles.

Rash's cough is better, he put in a fair turn of speed today... Without coughing. Paddy's' brakes are a little iffy though. It isn't often he comes steaming past Rash!

We ended up on quite a fast, busy road. We would normally avoid this, but we may not have a choice on the Ridgeway. Rash behaved impeccably (despite a depressing number of drivers that didn't slow down). Paddy unaccountably took exception to being passed by cyclists again. He was also more interested in what lay on the other side of the hedge than the cars speeding past.

Despite this we are thrilled Paddy is back to normal. The wish list is being filled. Thanks again to Pip from Hemcore, Catherine Jones and Shirley Milton. Don't let this stop you donating both items and money though!

Saturday, July 7, 2007

Rash's Turn

Poor Rash, he has the same problem as I do. It's almost impossible to take a flattering photo of either of us. In my case it's probably insoluble as you will never make a silk purse out of a sow's ear, but he's actually a very pretty boy.

We went for an impromptu hack with my daughter Kathy this evening. The original plan was that she rode Rash while I rode Paddy, but college and an essay put paid to that.

As she had finished by 6pm and it wasn't raining we decided to give Rash an outing and take May for company. May turned out to have lost a shoe (typical ****** horses). Plan B, pinch Bear. He seemed more than happy to be going out, but Pads wasn't too impressed to be left behind.

Both Boys were as good as gold, although Bear's little short legs left him struggling to keep up with Rash's rather extravagant paces. Rash has definitely got over his cold as he took every opportunity to break into canter.

Not wanting to tax the poor little chap (?), we kept it short and sweet. As we approached home a plaintive calling could be heard. Drawing level with the Boys Field there was a thunder of little hooves.

To my complete amazement Paddy was the culprit!! Normally, as he is the big hard boss man, he affects not to give a damn who comes and goes (so long as they show the appropriate level of respect for him of course).

There he was, hanging over the gate, calling and pawing the ground. He'd been missing his mates! Although he wasn't alone in the field.

Bless!

Tomorrow we are planning a pub hack (with tin rattling), if the weather allows...

Sunday, July 8, 2007

The Epitome of Elegance

Our ride was nearly over before it started today. A different set of dresses had an outing. Despite the aesthetic disadvantages of the other ones, the skirts are at least wide enough to allow sufficient movement.

These ones didn't! Shell's skirt got caught in an interesting way on the back of her saddle, trapping her leg (as you can see from the pic). We spent several minutes helpless with laughter before she rectified the situation and we got underway.

We did a very brief pub hack to The Sorrell Horse (thanks to the proprietors there, who sponsored us). More hilarity ensued as we attempted to dismount. At least people noticed us!

Went back via the 5 Mile Gallop, both boys very good indeed. We had to pass a pig farm, where Paddy did his usual 'to hell with this, I'm going the other way' routine. Shame I needed both hands for Rash, it would have made a great photo.

The bridleway to the village remains impassable, so we took liberties with the footpath (no walkers in sight).

Monday, July 9, 2007
Freaky Weather and Phone Calls

It's been one of those days! It felt a bit like we were busy achieving nothing. We still have to have to find somewhere to put the horses on the 18th (suggestions and offers welcome, we need somewhere in the Watlington area).

I seemed to spend most of the day making phone calls to Radio Stations. Three Counties Radio have said they would like to do a telephone interview... At 8.30am on Tuesday 17th. We will be in the Wantage area by then. With any luck things will be going smoothly and there won't be any swearing in the background!

Radio Wiltshire tomorrow (maybe). Fox FM in Oxford have offered to put a link on their website.

Thanks to all.

Last minute favours being called in, particularly in respect of a support team. Bike ride anyone?

I was at Tesco doing normal (non-horsey) things when I got a text from Shell saying there was a beast of a hailstorm passing over. Apparently, she couldn't get out of her front door due to flooding.

Being a responsible sort of horse owner (Ok I don't actually own them, but anyway...), I went off to check on them. Shell was worried that they would be battered to bits from the hail (hailstones the size of golf balls). When I arrived, they were all fine, if a little bedraggled. No-one does bedraggled better than Rash!

If we get this weather next week we are going to DIE! Anyone got any helpful suggestions on what to do in the event of a thunder/hail storm when riding on an exposed track (apart from not being on it in the first place)?

Tuesday, July 10, 2007

Sunshine... You are My Sunshine

We were a bit gob-smacked when we looked at Paddy standing next to George today. We have been thinking of Pads as still being a bit on the lardy side. His girth pales in comparison to Georges though! Yes, George is definitely a boy, so he can't possibly be in foal. In fairness, to the poor old lard bucket, he has been off work.

We are still chuffed with how fit Paddy looks.

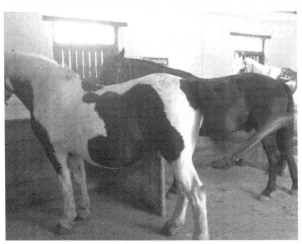

It was a lovely day, Sunshine!!

Due to time constraints, it was a short hack round the River Wall. We were expecting a swamp, which is what we got, although great care was taken not to let them sink and damage anything. Of course, we had forgotten about the cattle that we had to pass!

There was a very tempting newly cut hayfield on the other side, the gate was open and everything. We restrained ourselves though (mainly because a tractor had just moved to the adjoining field). This meant the Boys had to pass the Cattle, who obligingly rustled, snorted and crashed about on the other side of the hedge.

Rash was a big brave (quivering) boy and minced down the track snorting (and pooing). Paddy just wasn't having it. Cows are his pet hate. He planted and would go no further. Shell had to dismount and drag him! Once he started there was no stopping him though, and he dragged Shell the rest of the way past the field, barging up Rash's bum!

Apart from that I did an interview with Radio Wiltshire. I have a feeling I just jabbered!

Weds, July 11, 2007

Ministry of Silly Walks

I recently joined the 'Equine Ramblers' forum online, as you may have noticed we are quite keen for a bit of company/local knowledge along the way.

This morning I got an email from Jenni Miller, who moderates it, she took our accommodation plight (on the 18th) on, and solved it! We now have somewhere to put the horses that night. She has been wonderful, as it wasn't a simple task, but her persistence paid off.

We were beginning to think that the most unhelpful people in the country were concentrated in the Watlington/South Oxfordshire area.... I think we were just unfortunate that we managed to find all of them in one go!

For anyone with an interest in long distance riding, Jenni's website http://www.equineramblersuk.co.uk/

Thanks again Jenni.

Shell was practising her 'Ministry of Silly Walks' routine today... Or possibly just copying Rash. From a certain angle, he does have a funny walk...

Gentle hack round the block today... We are terrified of pushing our luck and having one or both go lame so close to the start. The whole place is a swamp anyway, even the sand tracks are a mess.

The Boys showed every sign of being bored, the sooner we get underway the better,

We still need a support crew (read 'Week Long Pub Crawl').

Thursday, July 12, 2007
Exhaustion and Dire Warnings

Sounds terrible doesn't it? Well we are both exhausted. Shell had a barbecue for the clients at the Yard, to deal with today. I got off more lightly, just more bedding to pick up (Thanks again to Pip and Hemcore), and assorted phone calls and emails.

Our heads are spinning and I don't think either of us has had much sleep lately. There's always the feeling that something vital has been overlooked.

We are picking the Lorry up tomorrow evening. I think it will really sink in when we are behind the wheel.

As for the dire warnings, well Debs seems to think we are going to die, although not for any specific reason.

Apart from that we have been poring over the map and stressing about the road crossings. The A34 and A40 look a bit sticky, but we've also heard Goring can be hairy. Oh well... Too late now.

Friday, July 13, 2007
Friday 13th Nerves

No pics today, my hands are shaking too much to use a camera! The nerves are really kicking in.

I mean, really, WHAT THE HELL WERE WE THINKING!

Closer inspection of the map and conversations with Thames Valley Police have done nothing to allay our fears. At least they know we are coming (so they will be able to identify the bodies perhaps?). I didn't feel this nervous bungee jumping 600 feet from a parachute.

We are off to pick up the Lorry now.

Honk if you spot us in "The Turd".

Saturday, July 14, 2007
The Turd

Yes, that's the name of the Lorry. It's vast!

It's a fantastic Lorry, nice space for the Boys, they can even look out the window as we go.

Human space is pretty damn good as well. We were tempted to just camp in it for a week in Sue's front garden.

There was no chance of missing Sue's house when we went to fetch it. Sue had just come back from the service station, and was pulling into her drive. It couldn't have been anything other than "The Turd". Shell and myself simultaneously squeaked, "It's Huge!"

There was an event and barbecue for the children at the Yard this morning, so we haven't had a chance to load the Boys and see what they think (not that they have a choice).

We have all the bits and pieces more or less assembled and ready to load, although I can't shake the feeling that I've forgotten something important. My brain perhaps?

This is a much classier specimen altogether than our hairy horrors (Sorry Boys, no offence, but) ...

The sexy beast in question is Chicago, who is owned by Sue and ridden by Piggy French. We had a good look at all his pics, and left feeling thoroughly scruffy!

Never mind, the Boys will be following in his noble footsteps (sort of). We will have fun once the nerves wear off, and hopefully raise lots more money. Yes, that was a HINT!

It's hard to believe that this time tomorrow we should actually be riding the Ridgeway. I am hoping to keep this updated throughout, if Alex will oblige.

Huge thanks again to Sue Crane for "The Turd".

Part Two

Dispatches from The Front

These Blog updates – Dispatches from The Front, are basically Alex posting texts from Tess... Without editing!

Enjoy...

Sunday July 15, 2007

Day One - Texts Received

11.26am

Only just got Rash loaded, little bastard! If u
want u cud come and wave us off from the
Melton traffic lights bout 15 mins?

14.06pm

Halfway round M25 w8n 4 my turn 4 bog. All OK

17.40pm

Now riding Ridgeway at last!!

21.36pm

Survived first day. Dry but sore arses all round.

23.52pm

We ache n da bloody pubs r shut!

Monday, July 16, 2007

Day Two - Texts Received

13.13pm

Crossed M4. In Pub having restorative pint.

19.11pm

Crossed M4, needed drink! Horses not impressed. Passed Wayland Smithy 'n' Uffington White Horse. Hairy moments getting to horse B'n'B. Pigs, cattle.... U name it! We ACHE!!! X

Tuesday, July 17, 2007

Day Three – Texts Received

Dreadful start 2day. Did radio interview wiv 3 counties, didn't help nerves. Driving rain. Horses wound up frm spending night nxt 2 cattle. Pads bolted 3 times b4 we even got on him. Thanx 2 blokes from Nicky Hendersons yard 4 helping to catch him. Got underway, more wind n rain. Boys on der toes. A34 underpass intrstn. Going bn poor but managed a couple canters. Arr Streatley 6ish 2 lovely welcome n cup o T from Mrs Fenton, Stable Cottages, Streatley xx

Wednesday, July 18, 2007

Day Four – Texts Received

12.42pm

About to cross Grims Ditch. X

13.53pm

I want my breakfast!

14.27pm

Now we r lost!

14.31pm

We in front garden o stately pile...

14.34pm

Pads shat on it, now leaving in a hurry!

15.21pm

Breakfast @ last. Unfortun8ly it's a pint of cider!

20.21pm

Long day, left Streatley. Much traffic. Crossed Thames, some snorting and many funny looks. Path ran alongside fast railway. Bit tense all round but was Ok.

Bridleway much less maintained once off Ridgeway. One nasty road crossing. Miles n miles of no civilization. Got lost. Breakfast in layby @ 3pm ish. Cider. Pads spooked at merest whiff of pigs. Jumped puddle. Finally arrived at Lewknor. Now off to pub. Hope it open!

Thursday, July 19, 2007

Day Five – Texts Received

19.31pm

Survived another day. Got lost again, in the middle of Princes Riseboro! We knew we'd gone wrong when we hit a roundabout. Went up very steep hill, Boys slid down it on their bums. Nice lunch at Pub. Got lost agen due to crap signage. Lucky not to end up on the lawn of Chequers. Roads horrible. Stayin in Dunsmore wiv Juliette Dean. Lovely. Sore arses all round. Luv T. x

Friday, July 20, 2007

Day 6 - NO TEXTS RECEIVED

TORNADO SPOTTED OVER AYLESBURY. NO SIGN
OF INTREPID TWOSOME!

Friday, July 20, 2007

Made IT!! ALIVE!!

What a day!! Apocalyptic weather.

We are home at last, all of us exhausted. Far too tired to elaborate.

Will do a proper update soon. We are planning to write an 'Idiots' Guide to Riding the Ridgeway. Anyone interested? We'd love to hear what you thought of our escapades so far and what sort of info you want to hear...

Messages of Congratulation and further donations also welcome!

Huge Thanks, to everyone who helped and supported us before and during the adventure.

Loads more pics to come.

Watch this space!

Part Three

The Gruesome Details

So, there you have it... Tess's' brilliant Blog of the immense planning that went into our mad adventure.

I think if we had known how hard it would be logistically, and how much hair we would tear out, we may not have done this.

BUT I am so glad we did. It is one of my life's' great adventures (Ok so, maybe not on the scale of climbing Everest, or trekking to the North Pole... But in my little life it was a huge achievement).

Although etched on my memory, I have always wanted to sort it all into a book form (lest I forget in my old age!).

In these days of technology and Amazon, it is supposedly easy to make and publish a book... Hmmmm. We'll see. I am now on a steep learning curve. If by any chance you are reading this, it means I have succeeded, and our madness is immortalized in print!

At this point I would like to apologise for the rest of the memoirs... My writing being not a patch on Tess's, but I hope you have enjoyed the first part enough to forgive me. I just wanted to fill in the blanks.

And by the way, we raised around £2500 for Hollesley RDA, while having a ball (in those dresses it was the only option), and the Pig-sties were indeed turned into a decked area for clients.

Day One – Sunday
Home to Ogbourne St George

So, having loaded the Turd the night before, we were ready to leave at 9am. Paddy loaded. Rash didn't. We tried bribery, pleading, feed, lunge lines, prayers. And a lot of swearing and sweating. After all we were on a schedule. And we had 10 miles to ride after we had driven 4 or 5 hours to the start! Isn't that always the way with horses?

We unloaded Paddy, gave Rash 3 Horse partitions and tried and tried again. Patience was at an all-time low. So, I phoned for help.

Pat Craigie and Ed Daniell from Mike Daniell Driving yard arrived, sent Tess and I away for a coffee and a fag and tried again, with calm heads and a large presence (Ed).

Thankfully they got him on and held him in place while the partition was closed.

There was no chance of moving it over, so Paddy had a tiny space right at the top of the ramp, not that he minded! And so, we set off at last, two hours later than planned.

First stop was to pick up our driver Cheryl, who lived in a 20ft Lorry and was well used to man-handling it around town.

Having left Scrumpy and Buffy behind, Cheryl brought two much better-behaved dogs, and a didgeridoo for company.

She was also hungover and a bit blurry eyed, so I nervously drove the first leg. I actually enjoyed the journey! Especially the M25. Normally being a high-speed lane swerver, I actually found the 56mph limiter on The Turd very calming.

Just sit in the slow lane and relax! The girls did shut the doors that led all the way through to the Horses when they realised I was watching them in the rear-view mirror. I mean, why else is it there?

Once off the motorway, I had some seriously dodgy moments in some of those quaint Wiltshire market towns. Mostly involving narrow roads and on-coming traffic.... Which I tackled with my eyes closed. Don't tell anyone!

Finally, at around 4pm we arrived at the start of the Ridgeway (Overton Hill). The Boys unloaded with some relief and had a feed and water, while we took a few pictures.

Paddy was very wide-eyed at the hundreds of sheep everywhere!

The Start!

And so, at last.... We set off!

The first 10 miles was mostly ascending up a stony rocky track, which we fervently hoped would not continue for the whole 120 miles.

Many gates and sheep later (by which time Paddy had decided they were not worth spooking at), and as dusk was coming upon us, we finally arrived at Cold Comfort Farm. It wasn't really called that, and in fact we were given the use of a shower, and the Boys had a lovely field to relax in.

But there was something a little sad about the place. Plenty of stables, but no horses. Quite a lot of puppies though, not in the best condition, and we had to persuade Cheryl not to fill the lorry with them.

There were also rosettes and photos in the Tack-room, of what looked like a happy family... Although there was no sign of anyone except the bloke that owned the place.

Having walked down to the Village and found the Pub shut (at 9.30pm!!!), we turned in for the night with a coffee, and much speculation of the whereabouts of the missing family, making up ever more tragic stories!

We gave Cheryl the bunk above the cab, thinking she may get a lay in up there. Tess had a blow-up mattress in the stalls (Yes, we had swept them out), and I took the long seat in the Living Area, which I shared with the dogs.

Day Two – Monday
Ogbourne St George to Sparsholt Down

We left Ogbourne St George bright and early, after a quick bite to eat and a baby wipe French Wash. I have no idea why it's called that. No offence meant to the French at all!! Cheryl and Tess laughed as I applied mascara, eyeliner etc.

We had a better track up onto the downs, a day's ride of 20 miles (ish). This was reasonable going, and the part of the track I had once walked, that had given me the crazy idea to ride it one day.

The only problem is the Ridgeway at this point is open to vehicles as well, and we were pretty much riding in very deep tyre tracks.

We passed Uffington Castle.... Not actually a bricks and mortar type of castle, but a much older earth works, and near the famous Uffington White Horse.

We met a fair few people here that donated to our cause. Rash did an impression of The Uffington White Horse.

We also passed Waylands Smithy.... A Neolithic tomb basically, where legend has it, if you leave your horse overnight, it will be shod in the morning. Not needing shoes, we rode on.

But not before I had ferreted around in the long grass to find a box left for us by friends travelling in the opposite direction. It contained a donation and a packet of fags!

Apparently, Cheryl had spent a good while there, playing her Didge, and soaking up the vibes.

Just as we were enjoying the ride and scenery, we hit the M4 crossing. A fairly innocent B road: Bridge... with railing sides... and the roar of traffic was so loud it was like Armageddon!!

Paddy was pretty cool with it. We even went to the edge for a picture. But Rash had a complete nervous breakdown. Tess had to lead him, inch by inch, and I swear if he could have jumped on her back, he would have. A very nice lorry driver coming in the other direction stopped and waited as Tess slowly crossed with her Arab shaped back-pack.

Luckily just over the other side was a pub called The Shepherds Rest. The shepherds must have had a bad crossing with their sheep as well! They had stopped serving lunch, but we had time for a pint (to refresh Tess after her traumatic time), and some cream doughnuts, rustled up by Cheryl. Little did we know how stressful things were about to get!

When we left the pub (way after it had closed) we were in high spirits, as we had crossed the dreaded M4 (the Cider may have helped too!), and we didn't have far to go. Little did we know what lay ahead!!

After a pleasant ascent back up onto the Ridgeway, and over some undulating hills we then descended into PIG country!!

Paddy's most feared creature!! We had spotted the vast Ginger Pig as we came off the Ridgeway and he was already in flight mode.

As Tess turned to warn us there were piglets on the track, all she saw was Paddy and I disappearing over the horizon. Having pulled up and turned back, I stupidly thought I could lead him past. Oh Yeah? Ever tried leading half a ton of frightened pony in a long dress? Needless to say, he pulled free and galloped back towards the Ridgeway, as I struggled to free my feet from the entangling dress!

Luckily my whistles to call him back, alerted some walkers who caught him. I often wonder where he thought he was going!

Meanwhile Tess had found a road which lead to the Farm we were staying at. Sadly a 2-mile detour led us back to the same Ginger Pig... On the corner of the driveway to the Farm. Only one way to tackle it... Flat out. And so, we erupted into the Farmyard, dresses flapping, horses snorting!

Unfortunately, the Farm owner (a rather scary lady resembling her Ginger Pig), was already unimpressed with the Turd, Cheryl's' long dreadlocks and the dogs.

As I tried to force Paddy into a stall in a cow barn (yes, his 2nd most feared creature), she grabbed his bridle and gruffly asked if we knew what we were doing. With that, Paddy crashed through the door and nearly flattened her. She rather huffily gave us a field to turn them into and we hid in the Lorry all night.

Due to lack of a pub, we got stuck into the bar in the lorry (we were told to drink it). The Scary Pig Lady appeared once, banged on the door, said, "I see you like the Amber Nectar" and left.

When we went to pay the following morning, she refused any money on the basis that we hadn't 'used the facilities.' We told her we hadn't known there was any. Whereupon she snorted, "Of course there are. What do you think I use?".

We didn't like to mention we had peed in her Hay Barn all night!!

Day Three – Tuesday

Sparsholt Down to Streatley

Tess had to do a quick (and nerve-wracking) interview live on some Radio station, and we were out of The Scary Farm.... At High Speed.

We didn't even stop for coffee. We just tacked up and galloped on out. Literally!!

Cheryl found a parking area just off the Ridgeway a couple of miles away, and we gave the Boys their breakfast, got dressed, and our breath back. Literally mid bacon sandwich, Cheryl suddenly announced that Paddy had gone.

Yes, I legged it up the road in that dress, to meet Paddy coming back, calmly led by a very tall chap, and looking for all the world like a child's pony. The helpful guy was from Nicky Henderson Racing Stable, and when I told him what we were doing and where we had spent the night, he laughed heartily and said he would run away from there too! Apparently the "Pig Lady" is known for being a bit 'eccentric'.

We then embarked on another 20-mile trek. Probably the most boring of the days. Miles and miles and miles of bleak downs. Made bleaker still by wind and rain.

Occasionally there were Gallops, although Paddy was convinced the jump wings were pig houses!

Off the Gallops, the going was rough. Both Boys were on their toes. Apart from some very miserable looking children on some sort of Duke of Edinburgh trek, we didn't see a soul until Lunch time.

We met Cheryl and The Turd for lunch at somewhere called The Knob. Just as we had wandered into the trees, struggling with the logistics of having a pee, whilst holding the dress skirts aloft, we saw the second lot of human beings that day.

In fact, what seemed like a whole battalion of soldiers appeared through the trees!

And so, we set off into the bleak landscape once more!

At some point, we had to go under the A34. As I said, this wasn't a very interesting day, so it may have been before lunch. I think we were suffering 'Post Traumatic Pig Disorder' for much of the day!

Anyway, we were relieved to be going under the A34, instead of across, or over it. Strangely neither horse was in the least bit bothered by going into a tunnel. And we were surprised at how quiet it was.

Eventually we came onto a road that gradually sloped down into the civilization of Streatley. By then the evening sun was out, and apart from Tess suffering blisters on the bum, and the road going on forever, it was a pleasant evening ride.

Our host for the night was the wonderful Mrs Fenton, who had lovely stables in town for the Boys, at her home. We had to park the lorry elsewhere, but were given the use of a Farmyard.

Once we had settled the Boys, Mrs Fenton gave us welcome cups of tea... And even more welcome, the use of her bath!!

By the time I had got out of the bath, she had also given Tess a lovely sheepskin seat-saver.

As if all this hospitality wasn't enough, Mrs Fenton appeared outside the local pub, where we had had a meal (and alcohol!!), at 11pm to give us a lift back down the road to the Turd, as she was worried about us walking on a busy dark road. What a wonderful host!!

By this time, Tess and I had swapped beds... The bench seat wasn't long enough! Although I did steal the dogs to keep me warm in the stalls. I don't know if it was the cold, the slightly poo-ey smell, or the dogs, but I started waking up at around 6.30am (unheard of in real life!), while Cheryl and Tess slept like the dead.

Day Four – Wednesday
Streatley To Lewknor

Things got distinctly weird at this point!

As I mentioned earlier, I had begun to wake early. I had also ditched the mascara, as it seemed pointless.

So, I was more than ready to leave by the time the wonderful Mrs Fenton arrived to drive us back to the stables. Tess, however, had quite a sudden wake up call.

Feeling we should be up and at it, we told Cheryl we would meet her somewhere for lunch, and buy breakfast on the way.

As we were now in Oxfordshire, I think we both imagined having breakfast at some quaint village café, sitting outside, and holding the ponies in an Enid Blyton kind of way. Or at the very least, a pie and pop from a village shop!

Leaving the bustling town of Streatley in rush hour traffic was quite amusing. We had a lot of odd looks from car drivers as we sat elegantly in our ball-dresses at the traffic lights.

And yes, we also had Hi Viz vests on to add to the look!!

Crossing the River Thames over a long (well it seemed long) bridge was hairy. What with the traffic and the unintended half-passing, we were glad to finally get off the busy roads onto a narrow track over-looking the Thames down a 200ft drop.

Until we realised that the track ran alongside the railway line, and every 10 minutes a train rushed past, London bound. Every 10 minutes I thought I would end up dead in the Thames, as Paddy panicked. After about 10 miles we finally went under the track, through a tunnel, and timed it between trains.

However, we were no longer allowed on the Ridgeway itself, as it inexplicably becomes a footpath, so we had to follow The Icknield Way, which has zero signposts!!

Or Village shops! Or Villages! We had half a bottle of water and a packet of polos between us. On we rode, down deserted country lanes, and through a dump. The horses were luckier than us, drinking from puddles and snacking on grass.

Cheryl phoned to say she had found a Pub. Our hopes were dashed as the Pub refused to let us bring the horses!!! Slightly ironic, as it was called The Three Horseshoes!!!

At one point we got very lost, and ended up in the garden of a stately pile, where Paddy felt the need to poo, before we legged it down the drive. At least the gates at the bottom were open!

Eventually at about 4pm, and dying of hunger and thirst (it was a hot day of course!), we finally joined the Ridgeway again. The lovely Cheryl had parked in the first stop available and walked to meet us, with the only liquid refreshment left on the Lorry... Yup two cans of extra strong cider!!

Eventually we got it together enough to ride the last 5 miles of the day... Although our heads were spinning!! And we were unsure of the direction!

Luckily, we had an easy ride, except for entering Lewknor. We thought the traffic was heavy, then we realised we were crossing a slip road to the M40, AND we had to go down a set of steps the other side.

Naturally, we went to look for the Pub before finding our accommodation, which was very posh. I think we lowered the tone somewhat!

This was the private accommodation that had been found for us through a friend of a friend, of a friend of the kind lady Jenni, who took it upon herself to help us.

We were given lovely stables in the grounds of an equally lovely house. As Paddy had been known to frequently leave stables once the door was open half an inch, we were not taking any chances! So, I untacked him, removed my dress and handed the stuff to Tess over the door. She then passed me feed, hay and water, and I climbed out over the door.

We spent the early part of the evening in the Pub... Not to drink I hasten to add. All our use of pubs makes this sound like a glorified Pub crawl!!! But we were actually eating at them. We had promised ourselves that we would eat well, and treat Cheryl at least once a day, to a decent meal. This all came out of our own pockets, and not the donations!

Sadly, I don't remember the name of this Pub, but I do remember the best Sausage, Mash and Onion Gravy I have ever had.

Day Five – Thursday

Lewknor to Dunsmore

Once again, I was up before the birds, and mooched about a bit, before feeding the horses.

We managed to muck out and tack up without losing Paddy, and said a grateful goodbye to our hosts. Grateful for both their hospitality, and the fact Paddy hadn't run amok amongst their manicured lawns!

This was a day of getting lost!!

First off, we had to cross the M40.

We were relieved to find a tunnel under it, what with the horses being experts at tunnels!

Then we had a really fast A road to cross.

We sat waiting for a gap in the 70mph traffic before pounding across at a very extended trot!

Things got distinctly urban!

We ended up in the middle of Princes Risborough! A small, but very busy market town. We made our way through a crowded town centre, squeezing between trucks and the path. Paddy spooked at every single rubbish bin, into the trucks which are not at all scary!

I swear Rash did the whole thing with his eyes closed and his nosed firmly glued to Paddy's' tail. We realised we were lost when we came to a roundabout which lead to a dual carriageway!

And so, we retraced our steps... By this time quite a crowd had gathered to watch the strange overdressed horse riders. We were too embarrassed to ask for money, so we smiled serenely as if it were the most normal thing in the world to be doing!

Finally, we found the track, which incidentally was close to the edge of town. In fact, how we missed it is a mystery!

We must have been on our phones, napping, or looking at maps.

Tess got very adept at laying the map out on Ryscheyed's' neck (the map reading didn't improve though!!)

The correct track led up into the woods which was a lovely cool relief after bleak downs and busy towns!

And down a vertical hill, to the pub Cheryl had found for lunch. Tess and Rash went first, sliding down with the splayed legs of a cartoon character. I led Paddy down, one foot at a time, terrified he would hurt himself, and somehow, we all slithered into the Pub carpark with minutes to spare for lunch!

Of course, we attracted a lot of attention, and more donations. It was lovely to sit outside stuffing chips, while the Boys munched hay at the Lorry. It's odd how quickly life like this becomes very normal.

After leaving the Pub, we found ourselves on a very busy road, while looking for an obvious track through the woods. As cars whizzed past at 50mph plus, and after about half an hour, we realised we must have overshot the track... again!

Having back-tracked and studied the map, we entered the woods, in the only possible place.

The track however was overgrown to the point of being an impassable jungle. Luckily Tess had a knife on her... Possibly Girl Scout tendencies, or possibly to kill me... Or Rash... Or Paddy... Or all of us!!

We hacked our way through. And popped out in front of Chequers front gates... Like you do!!

After showing a bit of leg, and begging for money (to no avail), we set off again.

We finished the day with a pleasant ride through more woods to Dunsmore. The ponies had a lovely paddock and we were offered the use of a "Summerhouse", which turned out to be a brilliant log cabin, which we all moved into pronto. It was with squeals of joy we discovered running water, beds and sofas!! And a toilet!! Small pleasures.

Things unravelled a bit after that!!

Firstly, we were interviewed by the local press who told us they were on flood watch the following day!?!

We were then taken for a pub meal by some friends of Tess, and joined by friends of mine. One drink followed another!

It was like the last day of school!! Back at the Summerhouse with my friends, we partied long and hard all night!

We had wayyy too much to drink!!

Day Six – Friday
Dunsmore to Home

The last day dawned with torrential rain, thunderstorms and hangovers!!

As the Boys stood having breakfast, looking miserable in rugs, we considered quitting.

Then our cheerful host announced her and her boys were off for a hack. Not to be out-done by children, we girded our hungover loins and set out to complete the last 10 miles. Without the dresses... The weather was so bad, and the Boys so bedraggled to start with, we didn't want to weigh ourselves down with soggy dresses.

The first half hour through the woods wasn't so bad. We at least had a bit of shelter.

We also had young cows hanging over the path, which did nothing to improve Paddy's' mood.

As the path was narrow and flanked by a low stock fence, and a sheer drop, we had to keep moving forward. At the gate we had to rush headlong through, due to all the cows leaning over to say hello.

Then it got worse! We ended up in another town, where all the cars splashed us. A thoroughly cross Paddy kept lashing out at the cars, not helping my hangover at all!! As I clung to his neck, chewing Opal Fruits which are surprisingly good for hangovers (other chews are available), Tess led us out of town via a housing estate and up a ravine!

It took a few goes to persuade the horses to go up it, having to jump a stream that was rushing down with some force.

Paddy, who normally wouldn't hesitate at such an obstacle, flatly refused to go on. Rash spun round and knocked over someone's fence. Finally, he took a stag's leap and Pads followed.

As we battled upstream with the lightning and thunder crashing all around, we wondered how the ravine was so deep, and weather it had been made by rushing water. We also debated the wisdom of being in such a ravine, with steep wooded sides, in what appeared to be two storms raging simultaneously from both sides. By then we were so wet and miserable, I'm not sure we cared too much!

Thankfully at the top we met the Turd in a lane that crossed the woods, and stopped for coffee and a change of clothes. Having rugged the Boys, we watched them chewing miserably on their hay nets, and pondered the point of continuing.

While we desperately wanted to stick it out to the end, the weather was extreme, and I didn't want to risk the welfare of my wonderful brave ponies, who had tried their hearts out for us, for the sake of 5 miles. Tess and I were willing to carry on to the bitter end on foot, but Cheryl, the voice of reason, pointed out that if we didn't leave soon, we would be swimming!

Seeing the Boys knee deep in rising water decided us, and we loaded up.

Or tried to!! Despite the torrential rain, Rash would not load, constantly flinging himself off the ramp into poor Cheryl, who was trying to stop him doing this.

Eventually I lost patience. The water was still rising, so I loaded Paddy, and said to Rash, "You have one more chance. You can either come now or live here by yourself forever". Of course, I didn't mean it, but thinking Paddy was leaving without him, he suddenly dragged Tess up the ramp and we set off home.

Mostly naked, apart from towels and dogs, as our last set of clothes were soaked.

The leafy lanes of Oxfordshire and Buckinghamshire were completely flooded.

We passed cars broken down in deep water, but with Cheryl at the wheel the Turd surged through, the Boys gently steamed, and I shivered away, clutching the dogs for warmth.

The weather didn't let up until we reached Chelmsford. We later found out that it was the worst storm Oxfordshire had seen since 1952!

By the time we reached Suffolk, the sun was out. The Boys were turned out into the long grass and we all went home for baths and sleep.

The End... And Many Thanks To all That Helped

There are way too many people to personally thank for their overall generosity, donations and help. So, a Huge Thanks to everyone that supported us in any way at all.

But extra special Thanks go out to Cheryl, our driver, chef and groom. Always cheerful and capable (and camera shy!). We could not have done this without you! Cheryl always managed to find us a meeting place. She put the lorry into places it really shouldn't have fit into. Being a much better map reader than Tess or I, Cheryl guided us when we lost. When we met up, the kettle was on, the hay nets hung ready for the Boys. Feeds were made both for horses and riders. Never grumpy, always calm and cheerful, Cheryl was our rock and the absolute best support 'team' we could ever have wished for.

Also, mega Thanks go out to Sue Crane for the Lorry. Without the Turd the journey would have been so much harder. It takes a special person to loan such a lovely Lorry out to two total strangers!!

We had a lot of donations, for which we are truly grateful. But the most outstanding was Stuart Durant, our Farrier, who not only shod the ponies for free, but also gave us a hefty donation. And Rackham's Feeds from Wickham Market, Suffolk, who filled the Lorry with diesel.

And thanks to all our horsey B&Bs, none of whom took any payment, and some who went beyond anything we expected with their hospitality.

And mostly Thanks to my ponies, Paddy and Ryscheyed, who went along with it all, and made me so proud.

And so, to anyone who has ever wanted to load their horse up and have an adventure? I say... Plan well, and GO FOR IT!

The End

Printed in Great Britain
by Amazon